W9-AUF-653

MEGAHITS *of* 2013

13 Pop, Rock, Country, TV, and Movie Chartbusters

ARRANGED BY DAN COATES

Contents

Anything Could Happen. . . . . .Ellie Goulding 2

Blown Away . . . . .Carrie Underwood 8

Carry On. . . . . .fun. 18

Downton Abbey–The Suite . . . . . .*Downton Abbey* 28

Girl on Fire . . . . .Alicia Keys 13

Good Time . . . . .Owl City and Carly Rae Jepsen 36

Heart Attack . . . . .Demi Lovato 40

Just Give Me a Reason . . . . .P!nk featuring Nate Ruess 45

Mirrors .Justin Timberlake 50

People Like Us . . . . .Kelly Clarkson. 62

This Is Clark Kent . . . .*Man of Steel* 68

A Very Respectable Hobbit. . . . . . .*The Hobbit: An Unexpected Journey*. 72

When I Was Your Man . . . . .Bruno Mars. 75

Alfred Music
P.O. Box 10003
Van Nuys, CA 91410-0003
alfred.com

Printed in USA.

ISBN-10: 1-4706-1023-X
ISBN-13: 978-1-4706-1023-4

 Alfred Cares. Contents printed on 100% recycled paper.

Anything Could Happen

Words and Music by
Ellie Goulding and James Eliot
Arranged by Dan Coates

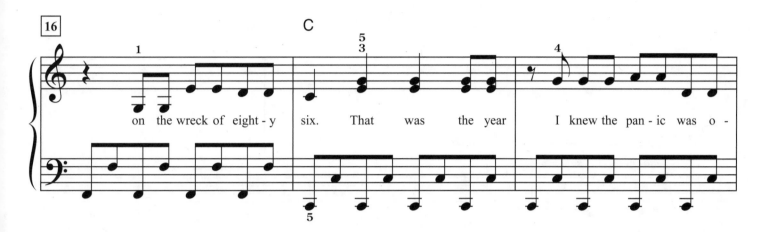

hap - pen, an - y - thing could hap - pen, an - y - thing could hap - pen, an - y - thing could

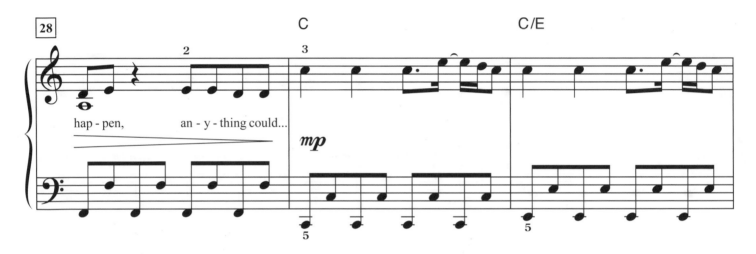

hap - pen, an - y - thing could...

mp

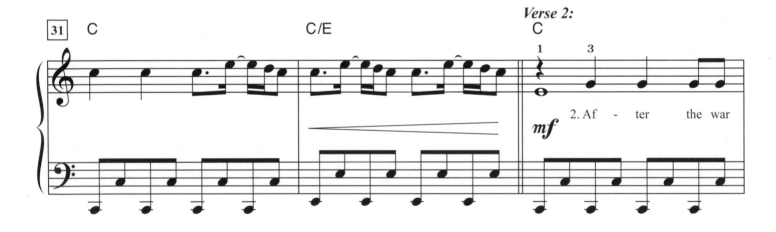

Verse 2:

mf 2. Af - ter the war

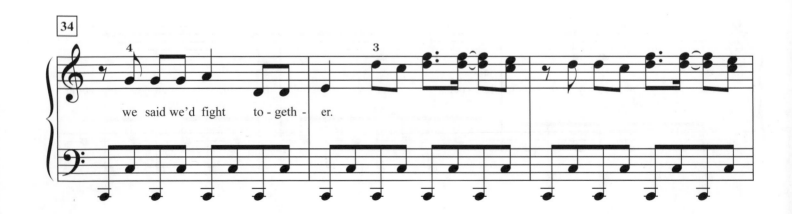

we said we'd fight to - geth - er.

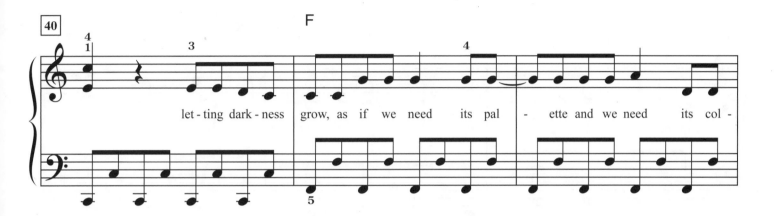

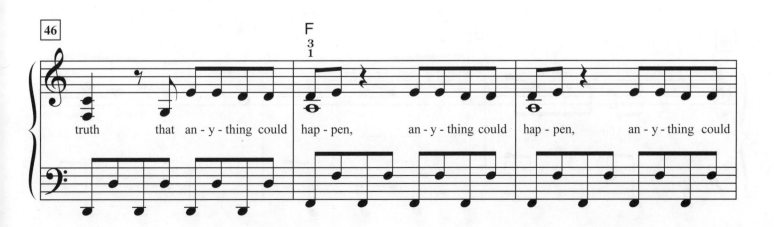

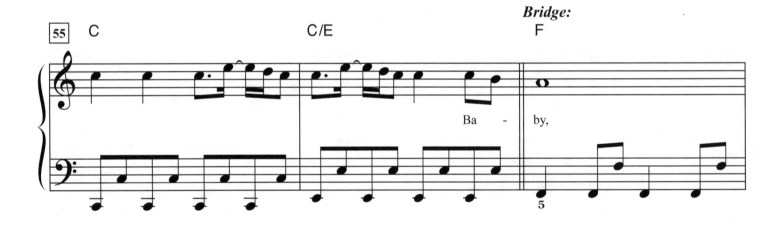

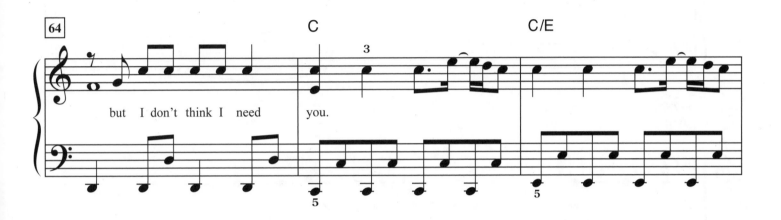

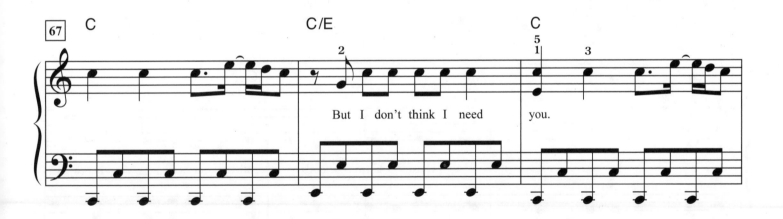

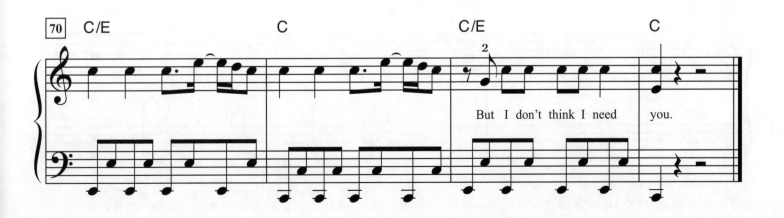

Blown Away

Words and Music by
Josh Kear and Chris Tompkins
Arranged by Dan Coates

14 mean old mis - ter. Mom - ma was an an - gel in___ the ground.

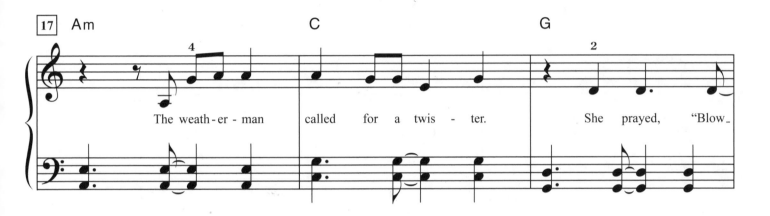

17 The weath - er - man called for a twis - ter. She prayed, "Blow___

1st time only

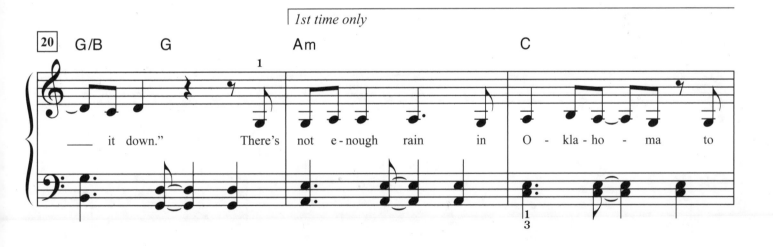

20 ___ it down." There's not e - nough rain in O - kla - ho - ma to

23 wash the sins___ out of that house.___ There's not e - nough wind in

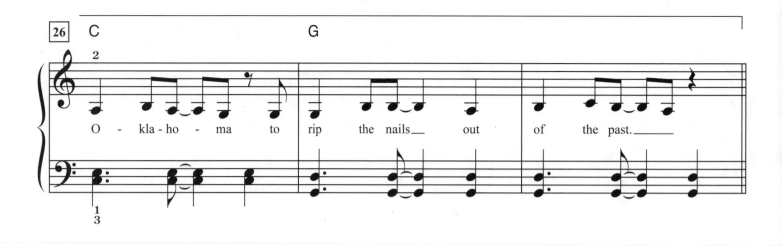

O - kla-ho - ma to rip the nails___ out of the past.___

Chorus:

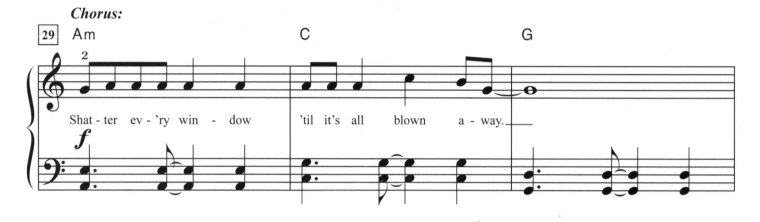

Shat - ter ev - 'ry win - dow 'til it's all blown a - way.___

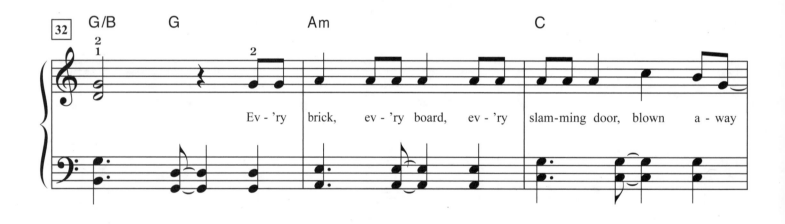

Ev - 'ry brick, ev - 'ry board, ev - 'ry slam-ming door, blown a - way

___ 'til there's noth-ing left stand - ing,

noth - ing left of yes - ter - day. Ev - 'ry

tear - soaked whis - key mem - o - ry blown a - way,

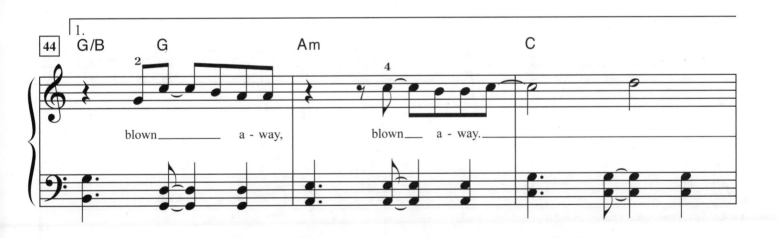

blown____ a - way, blown__ a - way.

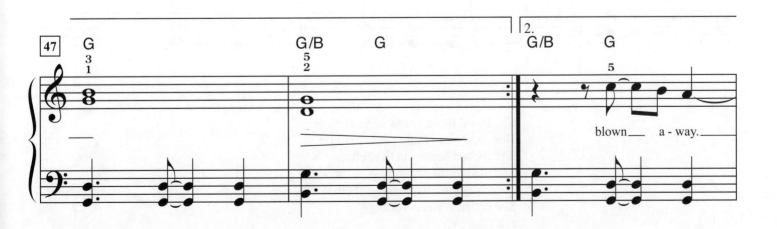

blown__ a - way.

Verse 2:
She heard those sirens screaming out.
Her daddy laid there passed out on the couch.
She locked herself in the cellar,
Listened to the screaming of the wind.
Some people call it taking shelter;
She called it sweet revenge.
(To Chorus:)

Girl on Fire

Words and Music by Billy Squier,
Jeffrey Bhakser, Alicia Keys and Salaam Remi
Arranged by Dan Coates

Moderately, with a steady beat
Verse:

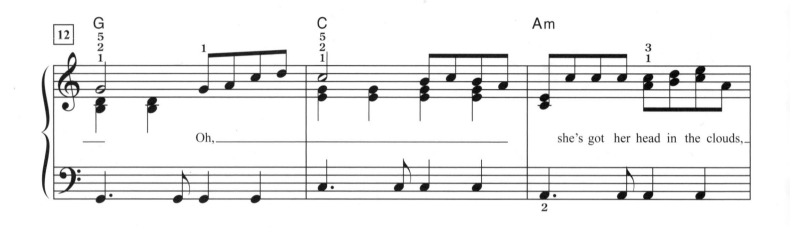

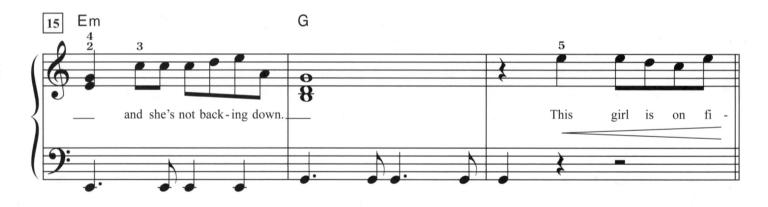

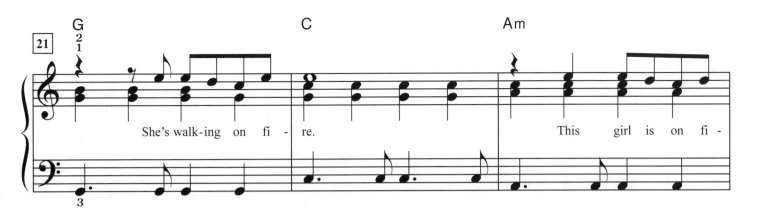

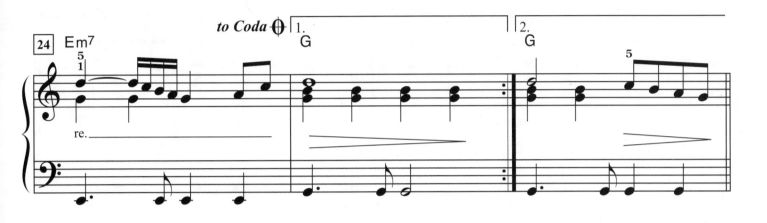

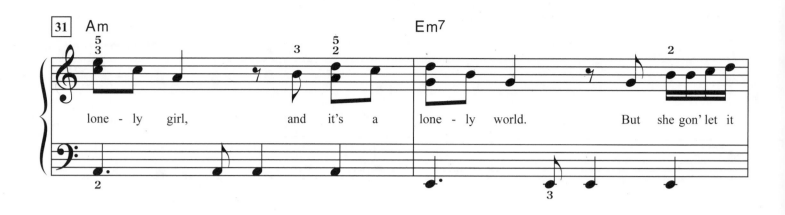

lone - ly girl,   and   it's   a   lone - ly world.   But   she gon' let it

D.S. al Coda

burn,_____   ba - by,   burn,_____   ba - by.   This   girl   is   on   fi -

Coda

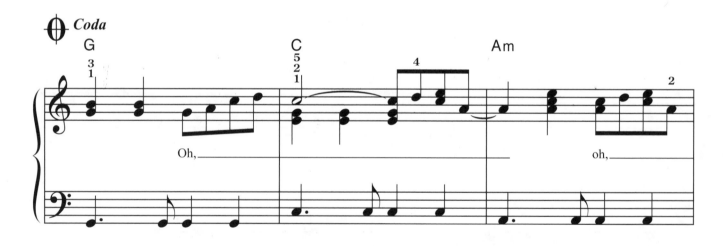

Oh,_____   oh,_____

_____   oh,_____   oh,_____

Verse 2:
Looks like a girl, but she's a flame.
So bright, she can burn your eyes,
Better look the other way.
You can try, but you'll never forget her name.
She's on top of the world,
Hottest of the hottest girls say:
"Oh, we got our feet on the ground,
And we're burning it down.
Oh, got our head in the clouds,
And we're not coming down."
(To Chorus:)

Carry On

Words and Music by Nate Ruess,
Jeff Bhasker, Andrew Dost and Jack Antonoff
Arranged by Dan Coates

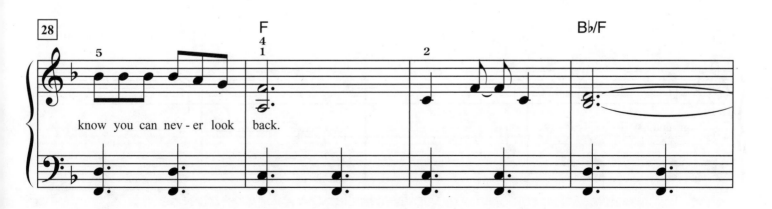

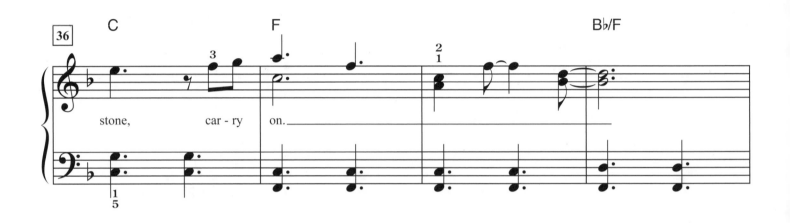

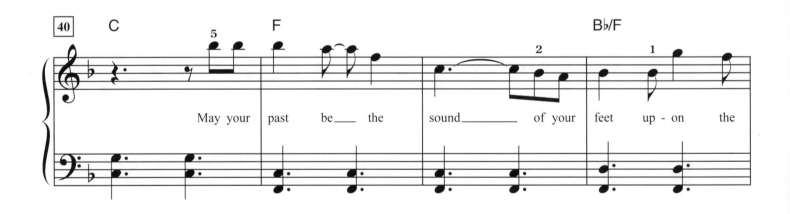

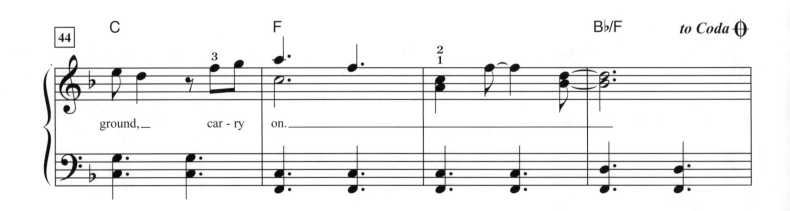

Car - ry on, car - ry on.

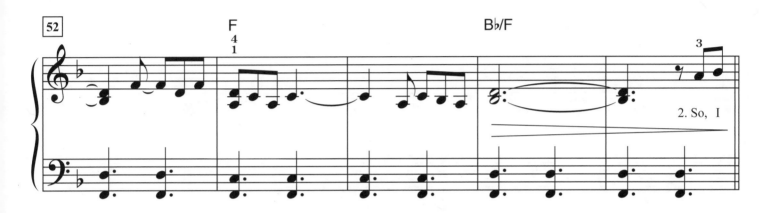

2. So, I

Verse:

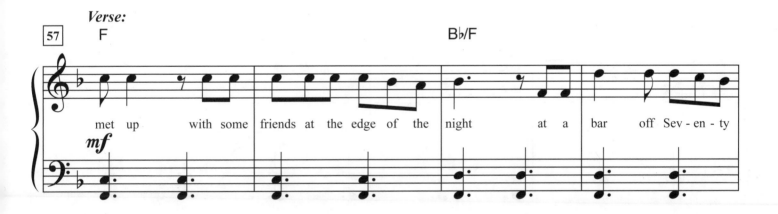

met up with some friends at the edge of the night at a bar off Sev - en - ty

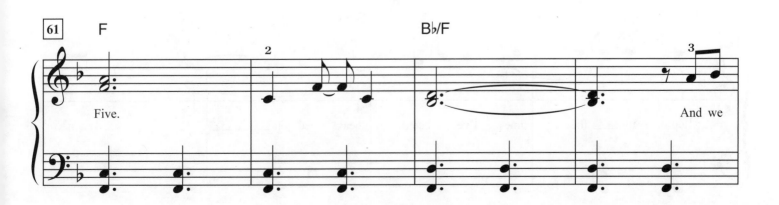

Five. And we

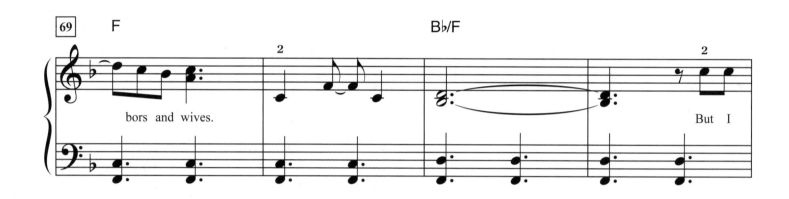

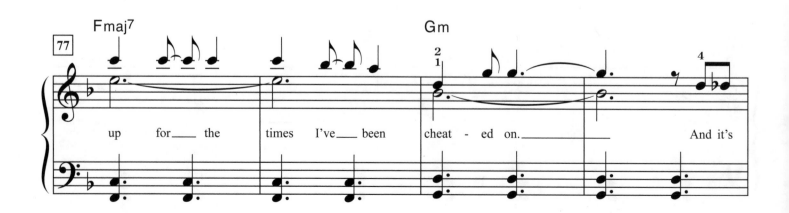

nice to know_____ when I was left for dead,_____ I was

D.S. al Coda

found and now I don't roam these streets, I am not the ghost you are to me. If you're

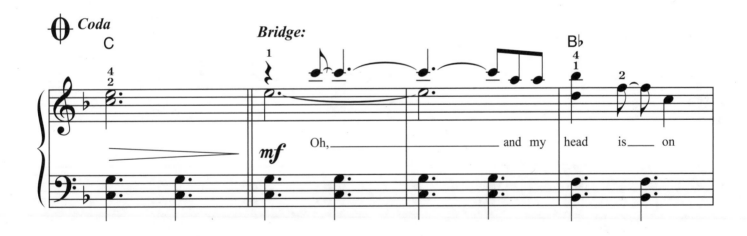

Coda

Bridge:

Oh,_____ and my head is___ on

fire, but my legs are fine._____ Af - ter all, they are

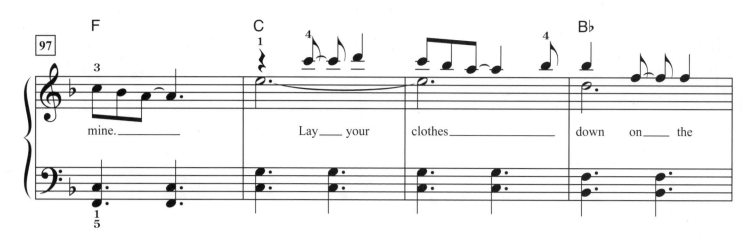

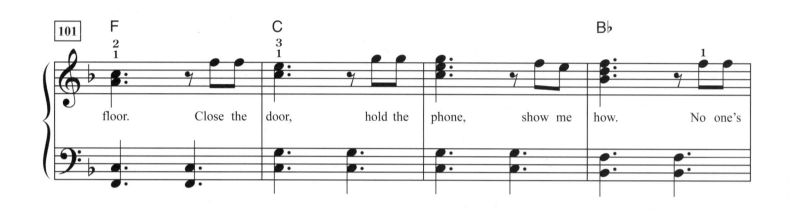

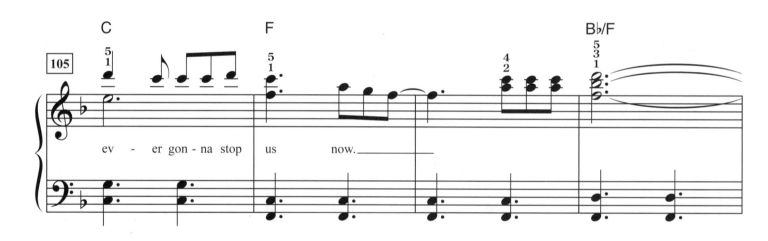

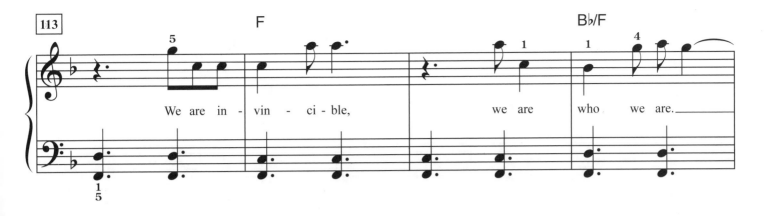

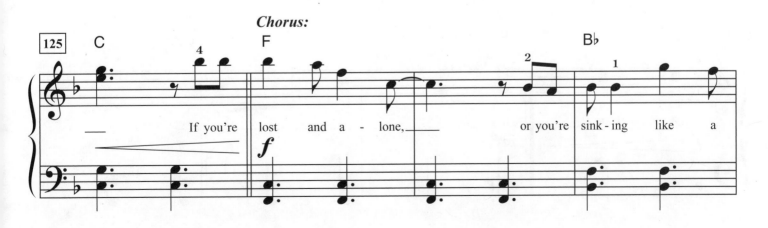

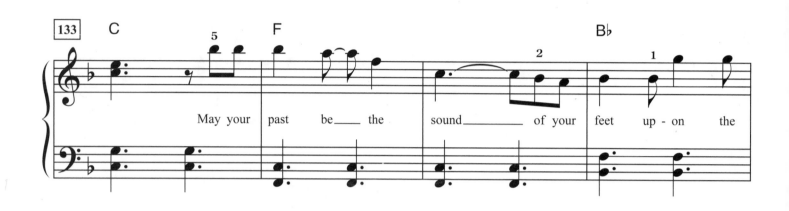

Downton Abbey–The Suite

Composed by John Lunn
Arranged by Dan Coates

Brightly, with spirit

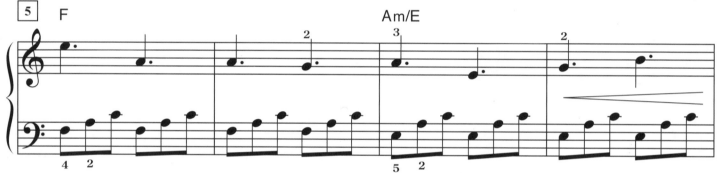

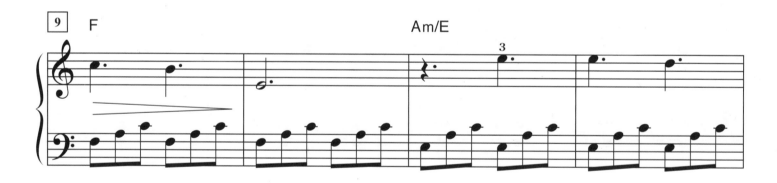

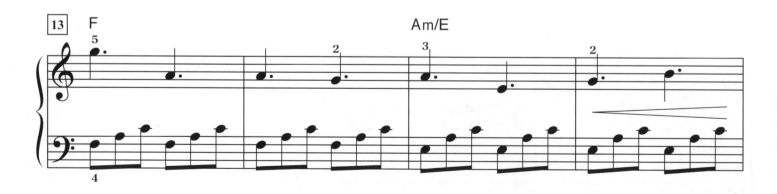

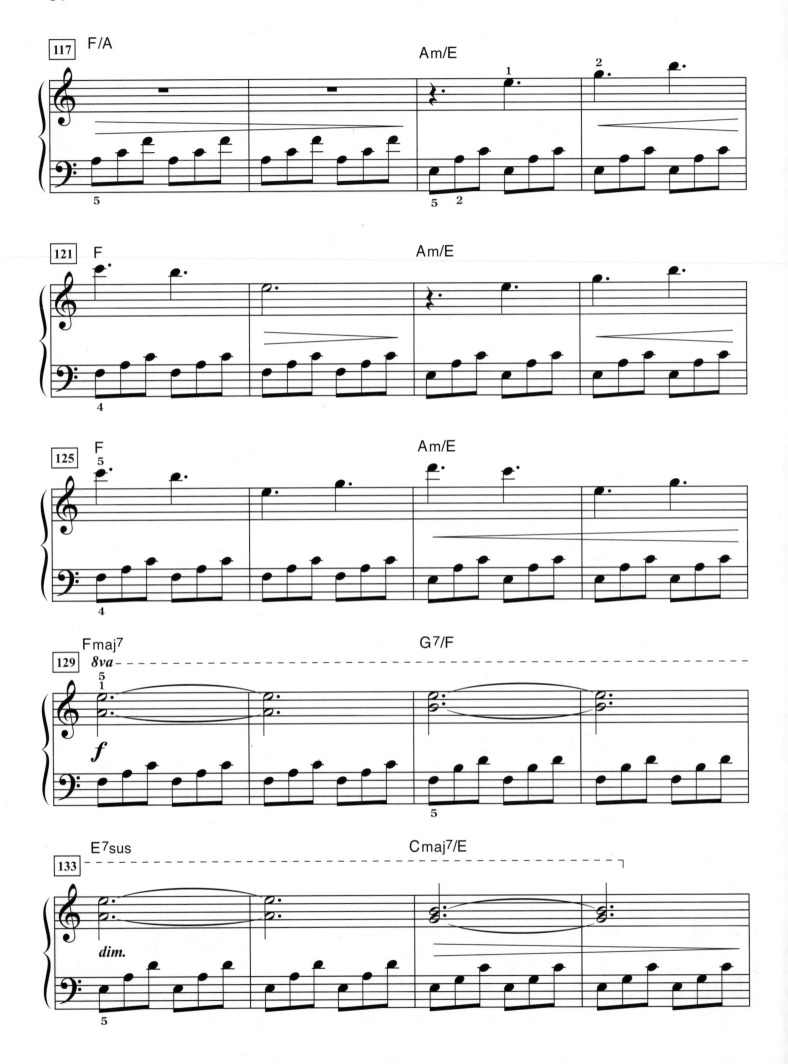

Good Time

Words and Music by
Matthew Thiessen, Brian Lee and Adam Young
Arranged by Dan Coates

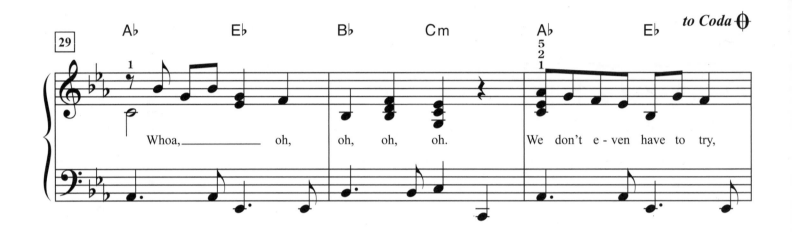

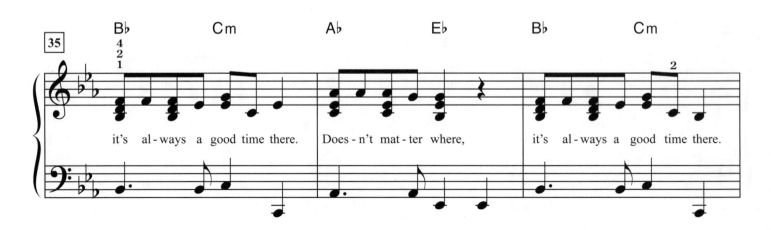

D.S. al Coda

Does-n't mat-ter when, it's al-ways a good time then.

Coda

it's al-ways a good time.— Whoa,_____ oh, oh, oh, oh.

Whoa,_____ oh. It's al-ways a good time.— Whoa,_____ oh,

oh, oh, oh. We don't e-ven have to try, it's al-ways a good time.

Heart Attack

Words and Music by Sean Douglas,
Mitch Scherr, Mitchell Allan, Jason Evigan,
Nikki Williams and Demitria Lovato
Arranged by Dan Coates

put-tin' my de-fenc - es up, 'cause I don't wan-na fall in love. If I

ev - er did that, I think I'd have a heart at - tack.

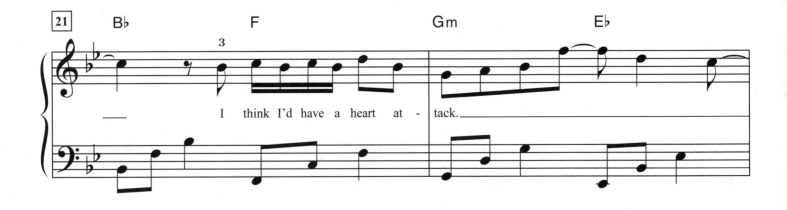

I think I'd have a heart at - tack.

I think I'd have a heart at - tack.

I think I'd have a heart at -

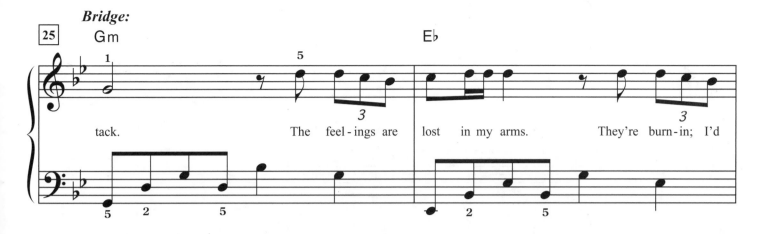

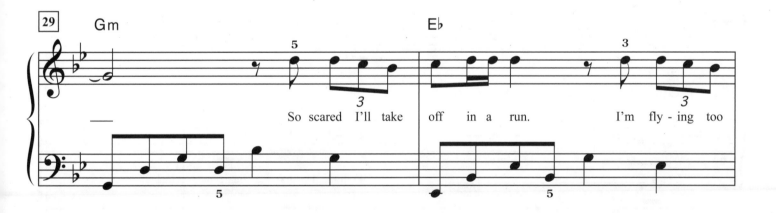

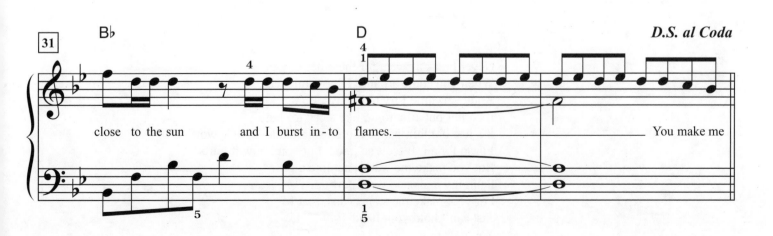

Verse 2:
Never break a sweat for the other guys.
When you come around, I get paralyzed.
And everytime I try to be myself,
It comes out all wrong, like a cry for help.
It's just not fair, pain's more trouble than love is worth.
I gasp for air. It feels so good, but you know it hurts.
But you make me wanna act like a girl.
Paint my nails and wear perfume.
For you, make me so nervous, that I
Just can't hold your hand.
You make me...
(To Chorus:)

Just Give Me a Reason

Words and Music by Nate Ruess,
Alecia Moore and Jeff Bhasker
Arranged by Dan Coates

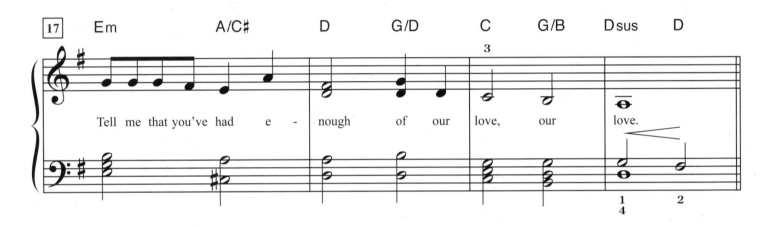

Chorus:

Chorus:

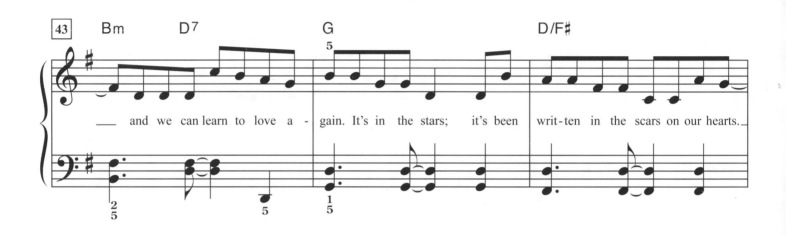

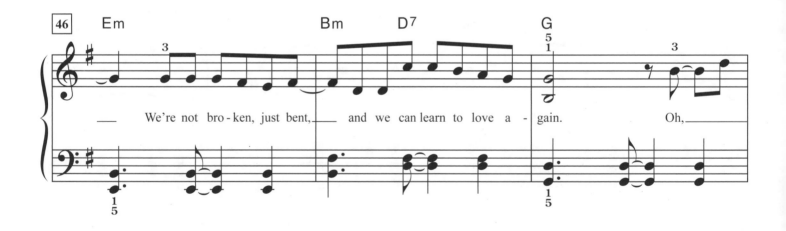

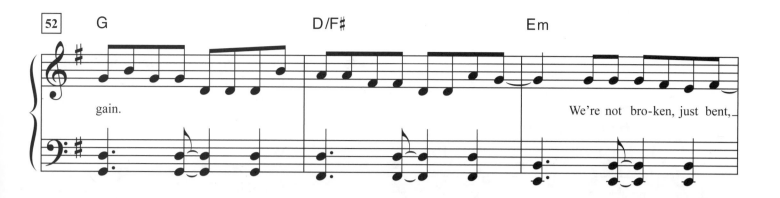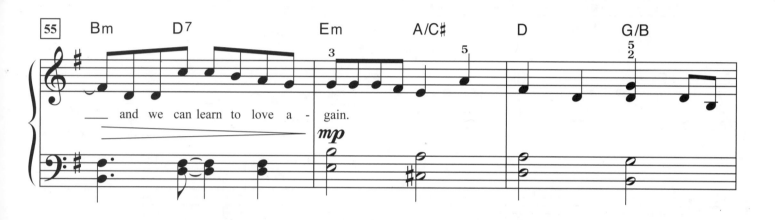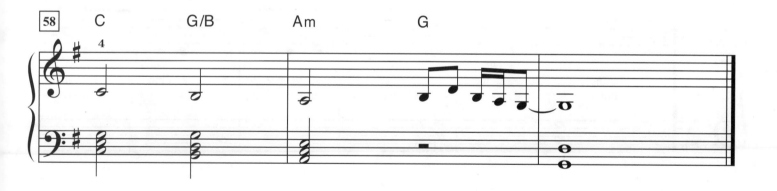

Verse 2:

I'm sorry I don't understand where all of this is coming from.
I thought that we were fine.
Your head is running wild again. My dear we still have everything,
And it's all in your mind.
You've been having real bad dreams, uh-oh.
You used to lie so close to me, uh-oh.
There's nothing more than empty sheets between our love, our love.
(To Chorus:)

Mirrors

Words and Music by Tim Mosley, Jerome Harmon,
Justin Timberlake, James Fauntleroy,
Chris Godbey and Garland Mosley
Arranged by Dan Coates

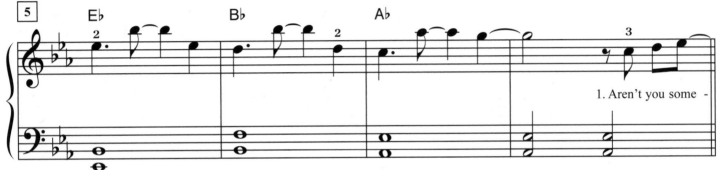

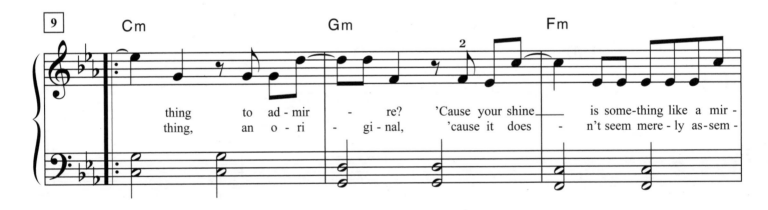

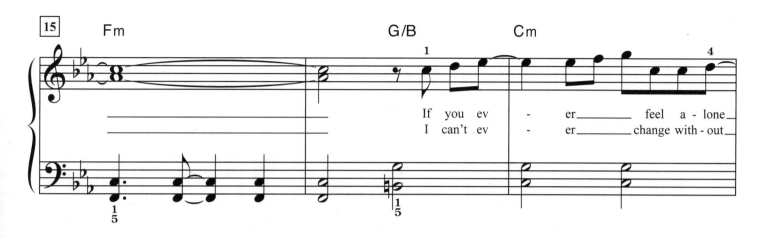

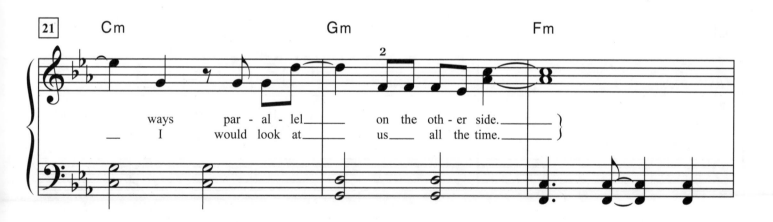

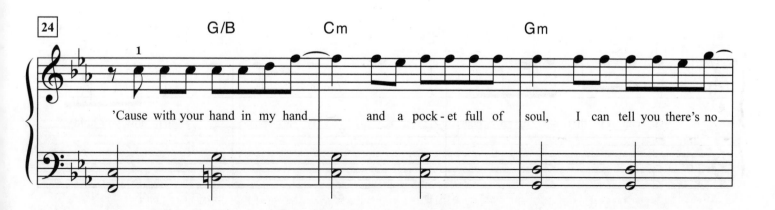

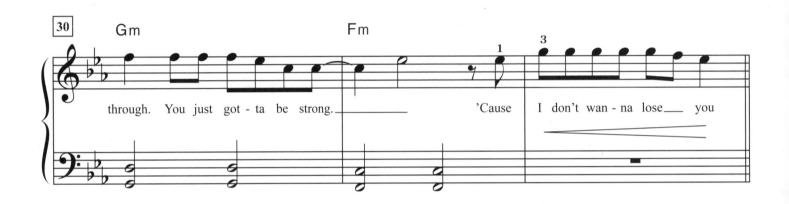

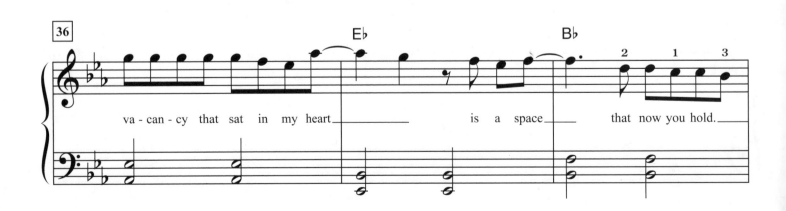

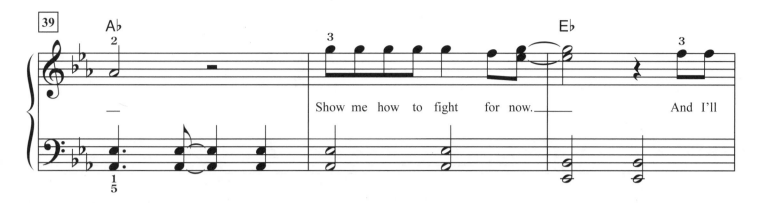

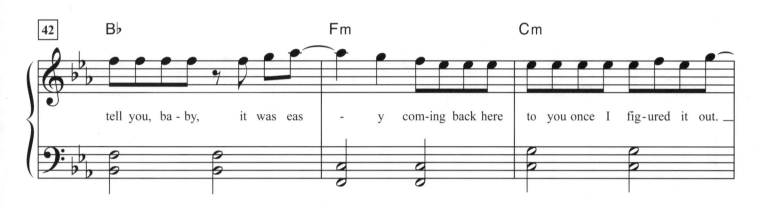

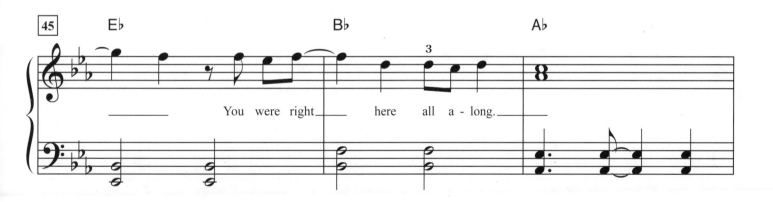

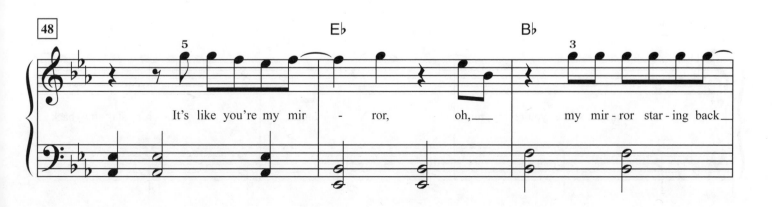

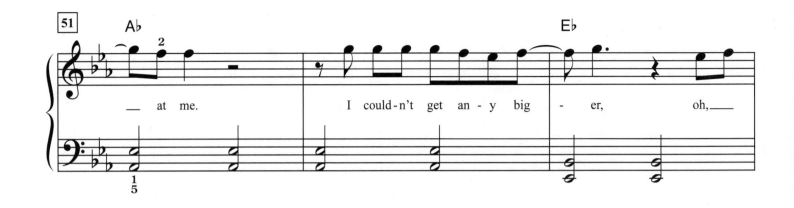

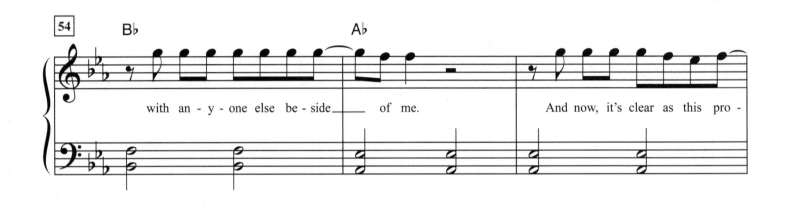

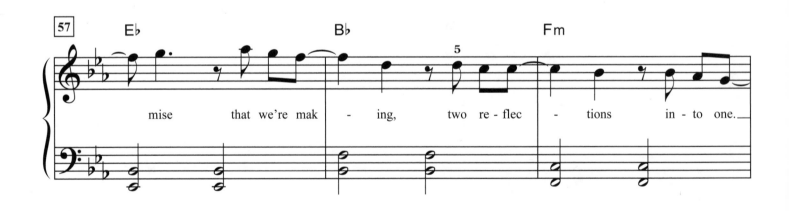

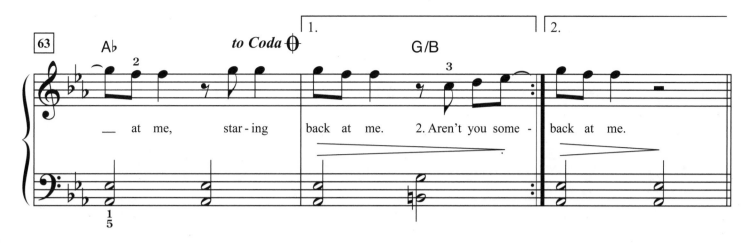

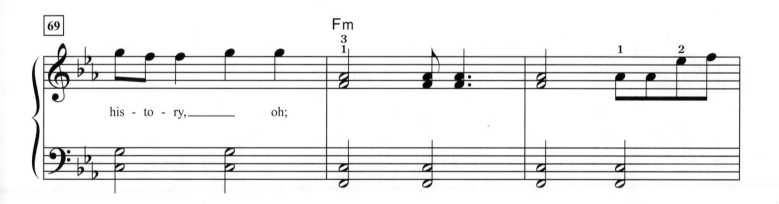

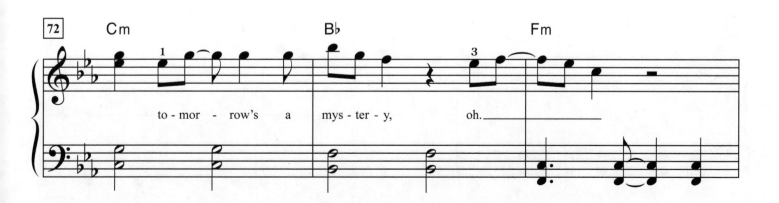

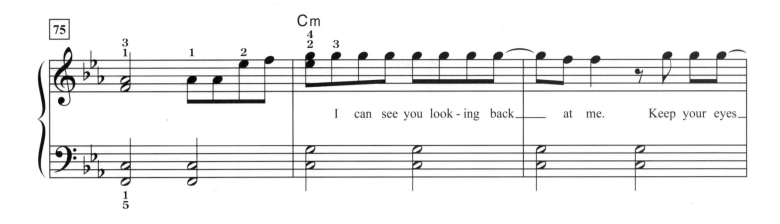

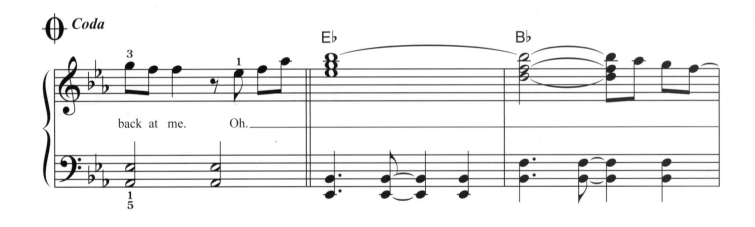

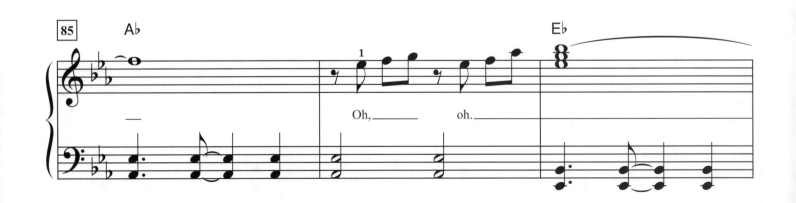

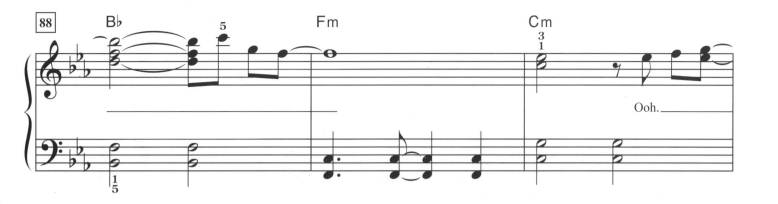

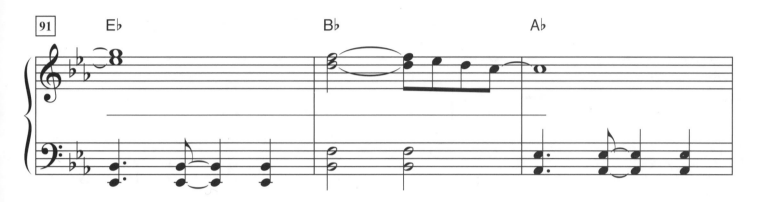

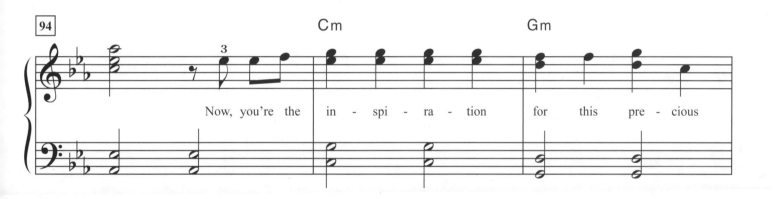

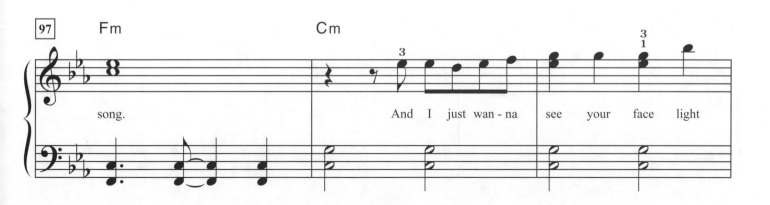

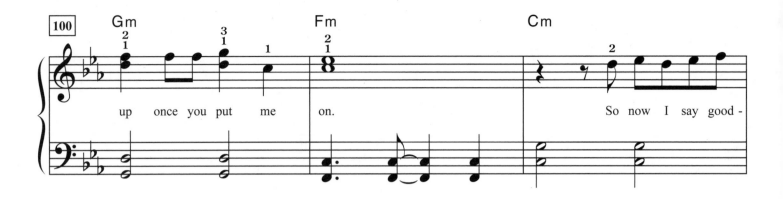

up once you put me on.   So now I say good-

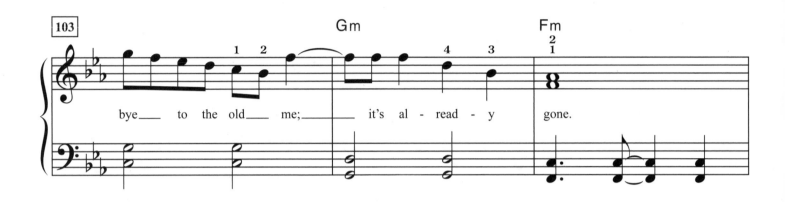

bye___ to the old___ me;___ it's al - read - y   gone.

And I can't wait, wait, wait, wait,   wait to get you

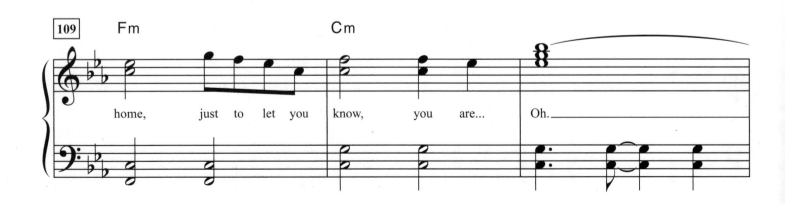

home,   just to let you know,   you are...   Oh.___

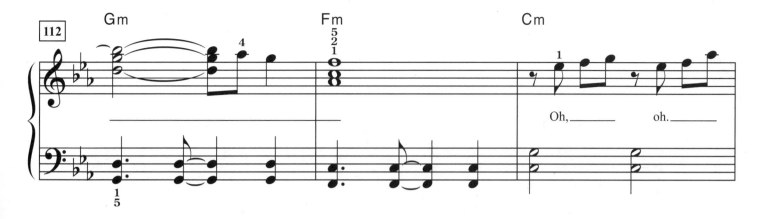

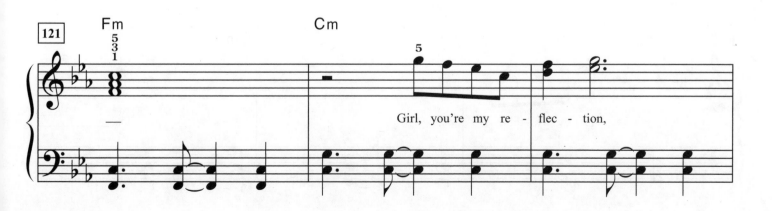

People Like Us

Words and Music by Blair Daly,
Meghan Kabir and James Michael
Arranged by Dan Coates

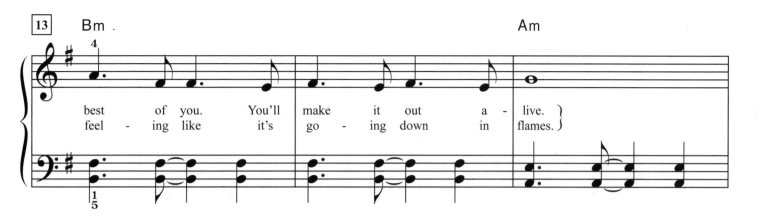

best of you. You'll make it out a - live.
feel - ing like it's go - ing down in flames.

Pre-Chorus:

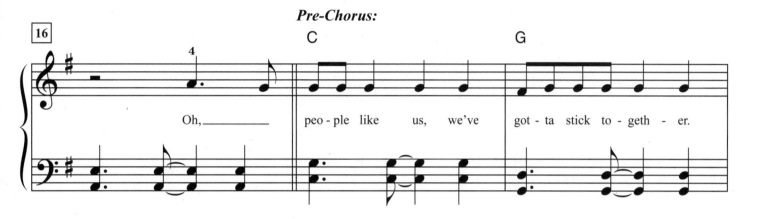

Oh,_____ peo - ple like us, we've got - ta stick to - geth - er.

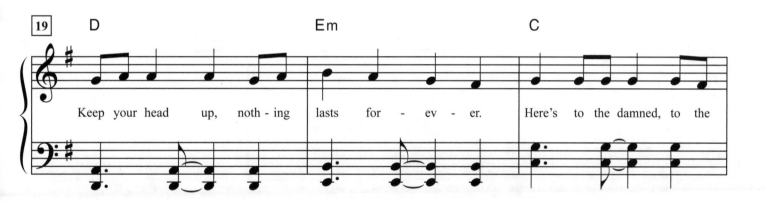

Keep your head up, noth - ing lasts for - ev - er. Here's to the damned, to the

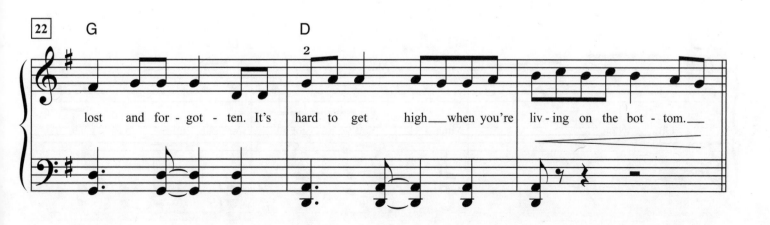

lost and for - got - ten. It's hard to get high____when you're liv - ing on the bot - tom.____

64

Chorus:

This Is Clark Kent

Composed by Hans Zimmer
Arranged by Dan Coates

Slowly and gently

A Very Respectable Hobbit

Music by Howard Shore
Arranged by Dan Coates

Rubato

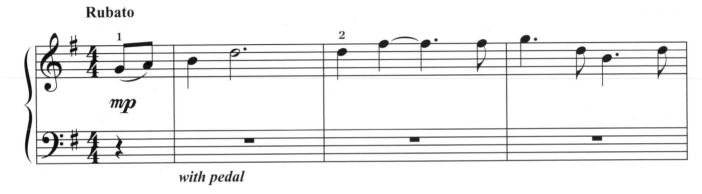

with pedal

Moderately bright

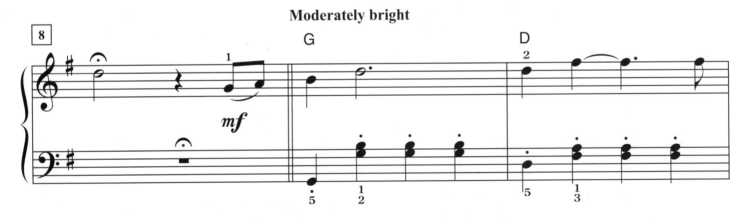

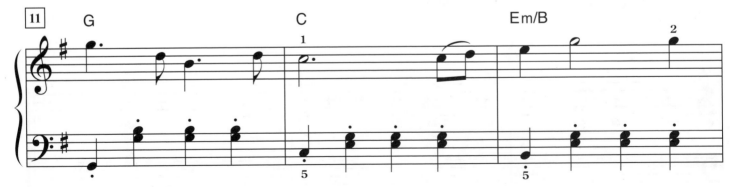

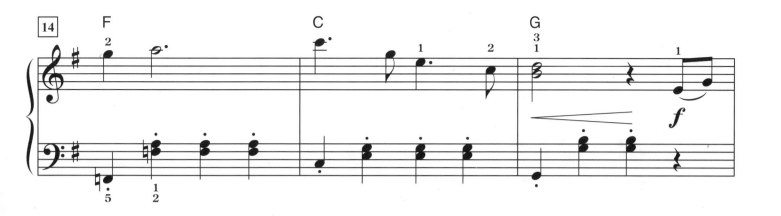

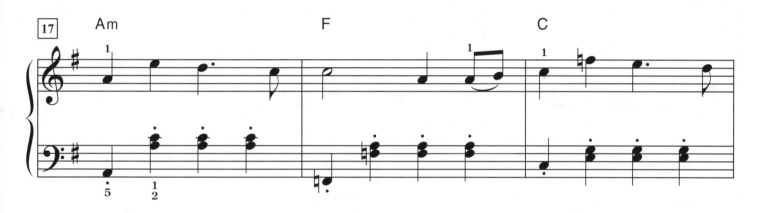

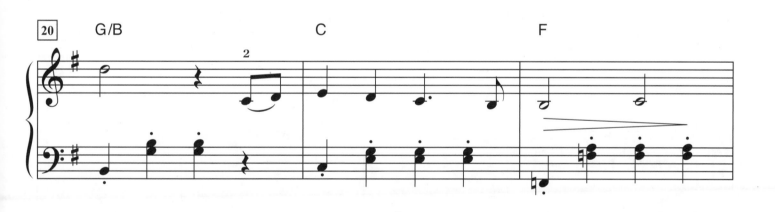

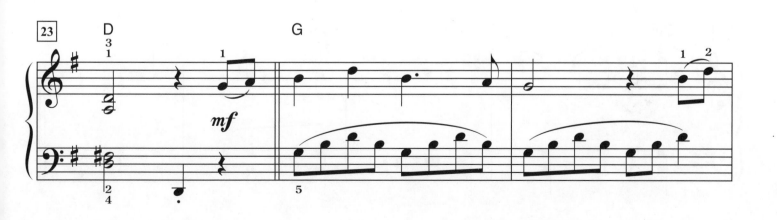

74

When I Was Your Man

Words and Music by Philip Lawrence,
Andrew Wyatt, Bruno Mars and Ari Levine
Arranged by Dan Coates

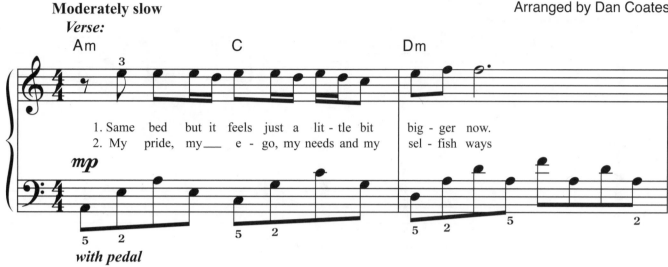

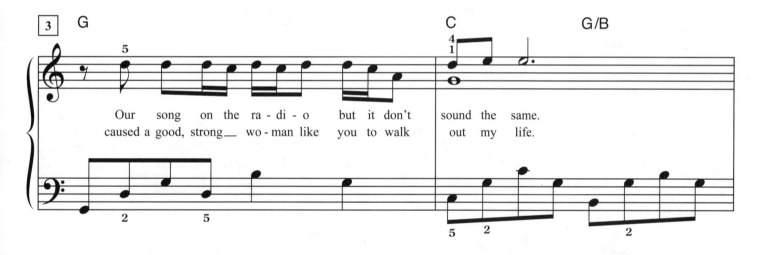

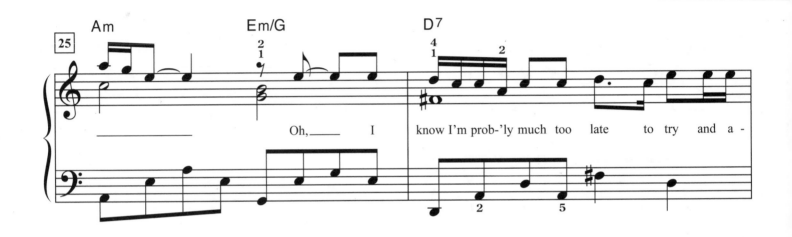